The
Spirit
of Zen

The Spirit of Zen

Teaching Stories on the
Way to Enlightenment

SOLALA TOWLER

WATKINS

Sharing Wisdom Since
1893

This edition first published in the UK and USA 2017 by
Watkins, an imprint of Watkins Media Limited
19 Cecil Court
London WC2N 4EZ

enquiries@watkinspublishing.com

Design and typography copyright © Watkins Media Limited 2017

Text and photographs copyright © Solala Towler 2017
Photograph on p 77 courtesy of Judy Mullan

1 3 5 7 9 10 8 6 4 2

Designed by Manisha Patel

Printed and bound in China

A CIP record for this book is available from the British Library

ISBN: 978-1-78028-990-8

www.watkinspublishing.com

'Zen Buddhism is a way and a view of life which does not belong to any of the formal categories of modern Western thought. It is not religion or philosophy or a type of science. It is an example of what is known in India and China as a "way of liberation".'

Alan Watts, *The Way of Zen*

Contents

Introduction

Zen is probably the most well-known yet misunderstood version of Buddhism in the West. Everyone thinks they know what 'Zen' means – some sort of blank state of being where whatever is happening is fine. Or perhaps the word Zen is taken to denote the core meaning of an activity: the Zen of Gardening, the Zen of Auto Repair, the Zen of Driving, etc. Yet, as any student of Buddhism can tell you, this is not true Zen. True Zen is so much more than this.

Most people, even those with a bit of understanding of Zen Buddhism, know little of Chan, the much earlier form of Zen that flourished in China 700 years before Zen became established in Japan.

Historically, the foundation of Chan Buddhism in China was laid by a strange and powerful teacher from India, known as Bodhidharma, or, as he is known in China, Da Mo. He is said to have arrived in China around the year 500 CE and his form of Buddhism emphasized meditation over sutra study and devotional practices (the more popular form of Buddhism at the time). Bodhidharma is usually portrayed in statues and paintings in China and Japan as an extremely stern, even gruff character. He was a no-nonsense type of teacher who even mouthed off to the emperor (see 'Bodhidharma Comes to the West', p. 46).

Bodhidharma's form of Buddhist practice did not exactly catch on during his lifetime but his disciples, or what are called the patriarchs, carried his teachings forward and within a few hundred years (not long to a sincere Buddhist) Zen or Chan practices flourished all over China and eventually in Korea, Vietnam and Japan.

Bodhidharma found so few people willing to take up his extreme form of Buddhism that he ended up sitting in a cave for nine years, facing a wall! (Whether this is meant to be taken literally or to symbolize the fact that he spent a long time there, history does not tell us, but it does tell us that he was an extremely strong practitioner!)

At the time, his teachings were considered weird if not heretical. As Bill Porter tells us, describing the teachings of Bodhidharma's spiritual heir, Second Patriarch Huike: 'he aroused the anger of other monks who found the Zen teachings of Bodhidharma anathema, if not absurd. How could we all be buddhas? And how could Enlightenment be less than a thought away, since everyone knew it took lifetimes to achieve?'[1]

Today this form of Buddhism is the most well known in the West, though there are many other forms of Buddhism as well, some of which, such as Pure Land, actually have many more practitioners.

(The other form of Buddhism most familiar in the West is Tibetan Buddhism, a mixture of Mahayana and ancient shamanic practices.) Bodhidharma's teaching was much simpler and yet much more challenging. As mentioned, his Buddhism did not rely upon sutras but was instead more concerned with a direct 'mind transmission' outside of books (words). He taught that 'Accumulation of knowledge is useless and clouds awareness.'[2]

This is similar to Taoist teachings emphasizing 'belly knowledge' over mind or intellectual knowledge. Indeed, Chan Buddhism was heavily influenced by the ancient philosophy and practices of Taoism and emerged as a uniquely Chinese form of Buddhism.

China has always been a great melting pot of various religions and nationalities and has been equally adept at immersing foreign influences in its ever-bubbling pot and coming up with a unique Chinese version.

The term *zazen*, meaning simply 'to sit', is similar to the Taoist practice of *zuowang*, which is often translated as 'sitting in oblivion' or 'sitting and forgetting'. A commentary on the *Tao Te Ching*, written during the time of the Tang Dynasty by the emperor Xuanzong, says: '*Zuo* here is associated with non-action, with a resting of the spirit in immobility, whereas *wang* means utter forgetfulness of one's own body. Thus the expression implies a double forgetting: the forgetting which is the method of meditation and the forgetting of this very method itself.'[3] This is a perfect description of Zen meditation practice as well.

For many people the most attractive elements of Zen practice are the non-reliance on scripture, the use of humour and paradox in teaching, the 'being in the present moment' attitude, the earthy simplicity of mindful practice in daily life, and the simple yet profound practice of 'just sitting'.

This is very similar to the teachings of Chinese Taoism, which had a direct influence on the formation of Zen (Chan). After all, Zen Buddhism is quite a different creature than the Mahayana Buddhism that developed in India and the rest of Southeast Asia. It was in its travels and transformation from India to China to Japan that Indian Buddhism became what we know today as Zen.

D. T. Suzuki states, 'Zen is the product of the Chinese soil from the Indian seed.'[4]

Another interesting thing that Bodhidharma brought to China was a series of exercises that evolved into what we know today as *wu shu* or martial arts (often mistakenly referred to in the West as *kung fu*). It is said that when he arrived at the original Shaolin temple, he noticed that the monks there were very unfit and unhealthy from sitting for long periods and studying sutras, with little or no physical exercise. So Bodhidharma got the monks up and moving – both for the benefit of their health and so that they would be less easy prey to marauding bandits – as a form of self-defence. Today the name of Shaolin is synonymous with amazing martial arts, and the temple is visited by numerous people from all over the world.

Bill Porter quotes a contemporary Zen priest concerning the connection of modern-day Zen to Bodhidharma, or the First Patriarch, as follows:

> External circumstances have changed, but external circumstances are not important. Zen is about cultivating the mind. The mind hasn't changed, and the way we cultivate hasn't changed. When Bodhidharma arrived in China, Buddhism had already been in China for more than 400 years. But people who practiced Buddhism then were concerned with the translation and study of sutras and the attainment of spiritual powers . . . But Zen isn't something you can see. It's how you see. You can't find it in a book. Zen is your mind, your Buddha mind. That hasn't changed.[5]

When Zen moved to Japan it was taken up by the samurai class, who layered onto it their very strict and often rigid code of conduct and ethics that they called *bushido*. This is the form of Zen practice that is most familiar to Westerners today and is most prevalent in Japan. It emphasizes 'just sitting' with little or no movement practice.

Here's an interesting description of the difference between Japanese Zen and the Chinese Zen:

> The differences between the Chinese and the Japanese ways of meditating tell something about each culture. While the Japanese tend to be rigid and quite formal in their meditation style and ceremony, the Chinese often appear more relaxed. Between periods of sitting meditation . . . Japanese meditators walk slowly in a single circle, sometimes at an excruciatingly slow pace . . . Chinese, on the other hand, do such walking meditation in a relaxed way, each person walking at their own pace in a wide circular area, swinging their arms and making a good healthy hike out of it.[6]

The ancient Taoist practice of *zuowang* sounds much like the practice of *zazen* today.

First one must sit quietly and get rid of all thoughts, i.e., mentally abide in non-existence and take no foothold anywhere. In this way one is united with the universal principle. This will next lead to an empty mind, i.e., a state of mind in which one is fully detached from the outside, to a mind of peace, i.e., a state of mind in which one does not turn toward things any more. Then, whatever one hears or sees one will feel as if one had seen or heard nothing.[7]

The first flowering of Chan in China was followed by a time of religious persecution in the sixth century. Because the ruling family favoured both Taoism and Confucianism, Buddhist temples were destroyed and the monks and nuns forced to resume their lay lives. (This unfortunately, was the sort of thing that happened at various times in China's history. Sometimes it would be the Buddhists who were persecuted, at other times it was the Taoists.)

Various leaders or patriarchs helped Chan Buddhism evolve in China, including the Fourth Patriarch, Tao Hsin, who settled on Mount Shuan Feng, where he is said to have founded the first Chan community. There, with his 500 disciples, he set up a self-sustaining, monastic community and instilled many of the qualities that Zen is known for today, such as the practice of maintaining the inner spirit of meditation, regardless of what one is doing. This included formal sitting as well as working on the community's farm, qualities that we see emphasized in modern Zen practice.

Perhaps the most famous of the Chinese patriarchs is Hui Neng, who followed the Taoist tradition of the 'wise simpleton' described in the *Tao Te Ching* (*Daode Jing*) as follows:

> Most people have more than they need.
>
> I alone possess nothing.
>
> Other people are brilliant
>
> while I know nothing.
>
> Other people are clear
>
> while I alone am muddled.
>
> I feel apart from them,
>
> like a windy and stormy sea.[8]

Chan Buddhism's history is full of such colourful characters as Lin Chi, of whom the following story is told:

A monk asked, 'Where is the true meaning of Buddhism?'

The master held up his fly whisk.

The monk gave a shout and the master hit him.

Buddhism was introduced to Japan as early as 553 CE from Korea. Then, much later, Myoan Eisai (1141–1215) founded what we know today as Zen. He was trained in China, studying at Mount Tien Tai, which is still known for its Buddhist masters today. It was there that he is said to have achieved enlightenment (or what the Taoists would call 'attaining Tao') and was made the official Japanese emissary of the true dharma of the Buddha.

Eisai returned to Japan and founded Kennin-ji Monastery in Kyoto in 1202. Upon his death his disciple Myozen also went to China to study at Tien Tai, taking with him his student Dogen, who would go on to become one of the most influential Zen teachers in history.

Today, Zen centres are found all over the world, including many in the West due to the influence in the 1950s of teachers like D.T. Suzuki, Alan Watts and the so-called Beat writers, such as Gary Snyder and Jack Kerouac. Many Westerners are drawn to Zen's seemingly simple yet direct method of spiritual cultivation. What many Westerners do not know is that in Japan Zen has become institutionalized and has lost much of its original simplicity and ability to go straight to the heart of enlightenment without a lot of religious dogma in the way.

The core practice of Zen, however – that of 'just sitting' – and its informal, sometimes outrageous fashion of teaching the dharma, remain in line with the ancient masters of both Chan and Zen.

So what are we to make of strange stories, like the one above, in which teachers abuse or even attack their students? How does spiritual cultivation translate into such bizarre behaviour as cutting cats in half or hacking off one's own arm? How can we understand such odd and even cruel antics of the ancient and not-so-ancient Zen masters?

Of course if someone is merely picked at random and hit over the head they are not going to attain any kind of realization other than that they want to hit their attacker back! These stories, however, are told about people who have already 'left the world of dust' and have put long hours into spiritual cultivation. In many cases the master can tell who is 'almost there', requiring simply a little more prodding, whether it be a koan practice or a whack on the head. The master is acting out of compassion for his students, not arbitrary cruelty.

Of course the opposite is also true. The master can tell if some students are getting 'above themselves' in their spiritual work and think they know what in truth they do not. They may think they are ready for a great *satori* (realization) or even enlightenment experience. It is really their ego that has grown, not their spiritual understanding.

In this case the most compassionate thing the teacher can do is to jolt them out of their complacency and spiritual egotism. The means chosen can again consist of a whack over the head or some other seemingly bizarre behaviour.

But only an enlightened teacher can read the enlightenment level of a student. This is of paramount importance. Arbitrary abuse of their students is not the sign of an enlightened teacher.

You will notice that most, if not all, traditional Chan and Zen stories are about masters and students who are male. Both China and Japan, not to mention India, are patriarchal societies. Very few women were recognized as spiritual leaders. Even today in many Buddhist cultures woman are often seen as second-class practitioners. (I even had one Buddhist teacher in China tell me that the most a woman could get out of spiritual cultivation practices in this life was the good karma to be born as a man in her next life so that she could then attain a high-level spiritual understanding!) Yet at its heart the practice of Zen, the experience of Zen, and the knowledge about self and other and about the world around and within us, transcend gender roles as well as cultural/historical divisions. Zen is as much alive as during the time of Bodhidharma and beyond.

Each of us has our own unique embodiment and expression of Zen. Each time someone sits down on a cushion or a bench and enters deep meditation . . . each time someone brews and shares a cup of tea with grace and humility . . . each time a teacher instructs his or her student on the Way . . . each time someone reads the old stories and creates new ones . . . each time someone shares how Zen has impacted their life . . . each time someone reads or listens to or studies the old masters as well as the contemporary ones . . . each time someone lets go of their egoic self and instead embraces their eternal self, each time someone shares what they have learned and unlearned on their quest for spiritual understanding . . .

Zen teaches that everything we see and feel and experience is but our own mind, yet that mind is none other than the mind of the Buddha. This is the way it has been since the beginning of time.

There is nothing to do, nowhere to go, nothing to be understood or learned or embraced or denied that is not Buddha, our own simple enlightened self. But this clear, wise being is buried under layer and layer of acculturated obscuration. When we are born we are clear and unafraid. As we grow we become less sure of our innocence. We become buried under these layers of duality and opinions, coming to believe that we know who we are when in reality we have no idea.

The Zen masters and teachers of old, as well as the Zen masters and teachers of today, wish only to help us shed some of these layers and reveal the shining Buddha diamond that lies beneath. And all the tools of Zen – the koans, the sitting, the studying, the chanting, the bowing, the cleaning, the working, the building, as well as the tearing down of the old and useless things that keep us apart from and ignorant of our true natural Buddha nature – all are useful and can help us reach that often brief yet shining moment of true insight and inner sight that will reveal the truth of how far we have come and how far we have to go . . . to enlightenment, to true understanding, to being worthy of calling ourselves men and women of Zen.

I hope the wild and woolly stories in this collection will help to inspire and excite the reader to create their own stories, their own insights and illuminations, their own attempts at letting go and getting off of the always enticing, yet ultimately entrapping, wheel of samsara, and to fly off into the outer limits of spiritual experience.

The
Spirit
of Zen

A Case of Bad Temper

A student came to Master Bankei and said that he had an uncontrollable temper, which he felt was obstructing his cultivation practice. What, he asked, could he do about it?

'Okay,' said Master Bankei. 'Show it to me.'

'I cannot show it to you right now,' answered the student.

'Well,' asked Master Bankei, 'when *can* you show it to me?'

'It comes on me all of a sudden,' said the student.

'Ah,' said the master. 'Then it cannot be a part of your true nature. If that were so you would be able to show it to me any time.'

The student went away and meditated on this and from that day his temper was gone.

A Curious Remedy

The old monk had been seriously ill for some time. He was too sick to attend the morning dharma talk and too tired to sit in *zazen*. All he did was lie on his mat all day and look up at the ceiling. One of the other monks offered a herbal remedy but it only made the old monk even sicker.

Finally he couldn't take it any more and he dragged himself to the abbot's room and knocked feebly at the door. 'Come in,' said the abbot, in a hearty voice.

The old monk hobbled into the room and collapsed in front of the abbot. The abbot sat and looked at him without saying anything.

Eventually the old monk said, 'Master, I have been so miserably sick. My bowels are in an uproar, I have no energy for anything and my thoughts have become darker and darker. I took some medicine one of the monks gave me and it was so poisonous it made me even sicker. Do you have a remedy for me?'

The abbot looked at him with compassion in his eyes but was silent. Suddenly he shouted, 'Gold! Pour the medicine on the top of your head', and struck him, knocking him over.

The old monk pulled himself back up, bowed to the abbot and walked out the door, feeling stronger than he had felt in some time.

A Lesson on Essential Mind

Once, the student Chongxin asked his master Daowu, 'Since I became your student, you have never taught me anything about essential mind.'

Master Daowu said, 'Since you became my student I have never *stopped* teaching you about essential mind.'

'When have you taught me this?' asked Chongxin.

Daowu said, 'When you bring me tea, I receive it from you. When you bring me food, I receive it from you. When you bow to me, I bow to you. When have I not taught you about essential mind?'

At this Chongxin bowed his head and stood that way for some time.

Then Daowu said, 'Look for it right in front of you. If you think about it too much you will miss it.'

As soon as he heard these words Chongxin awakened.

'How can I uphold this teaching?' asked Chongxin.

'Live your life in as free a way as possible, in accord with circumstances. Give yourself over to everyday mind,' said Daowu. Then he opened his arms wide and said, 'There is nothing sacred to be realized outside of *this*.'

A Real Miracle

Once, when Master Bankei was lecturing at Ryumon temple, a priest from the Shinshu sect, who taught that just by chanting the name of Amida Buddha one could be saved, came by. When he saw the large crowd of people listening to Master Bankei he became jealous.

He charged up to the front of the room and challenged Bankei, right in the middle of his talk. 'The master of our sect had miraculous powers,' he began, in a loud voice. 'He would stand on one side of a river, holding a brush. On the other side his student would stand with a piece of paper. When our teacher wrote the holy name of Amida Buddha in the air with his brush the word would appear on the paper on the other side of the river!'

Here he stopped and looked triumphantly at the assembled gathering. Then he turned back to Master Bankei and asked, 'Can you perform such miracles as this?'

'Perhaps your master can perform such miracles but this is not in the true spirit of Zen,' answered Master Bankei in a calm voice. 'My miracle is that when I am hungry I eat and when I am thirsty I drink.'

An Unusual Exit

One day, when all the monks had gathering together for a dharma talk, Master Dasui sat in front of them in his usual seat. Suddenly his mouth contracted into a painful shape. Alarmed, all the monks fell over each other, offering various potions and poultices, but all to no avail. Poor Master Dasui just sat there with his mouth all twisted around.

Once the word got out in the town, many of the townspeople came to the temple, offering their own medicines and cures. But nothing seemed to help.

Then, seven days later, Master Dasui suddenly slapped himself on the side of the head and his mouth magically took on its usual shape. Dumbfounded, all the monks and townspeople just stared.

'My two lips have been flapping against each other for all this time,' said Master Dasui, 'and up to now no one has been able to cure them.'

Then, smoothing his robes and sitting up straight, the master passed away.

A True Master

In the village outside of Hakuin's temple there was an old woman who ran a teashop. This old woman, Hakuin told his students, was actually a true tea master as well as a master of Zen.

The students, upon hearing this, were curious about the old woman and decided to go to the village and see for themselves whether this was so.

The old woman, who had studied the Way for many years, was indeed both a tea master and a master of Zen. Not only so, but she was able to discern from a single look whether a person was coming to her with an open heart to learn about the Way of Tea, or whether they were, instead, coming to check on her understanding of Zen.

To those who came to her with an open heart she served tea in a masterful fashion, and these left her teashop with wings on their feet. As for those whom she discerned were actually there to test her understanding of Zen, she would hide behind her door with a fire poker and began to beat them as soon as they entered the teashop.

When his angry and injured students complained to him, Master Hakuin laughed and said, 'I told you her understanding of the Way is unsurpassed. You're all fortunate that she let you leave in one piece!'

Bankei's Realization

Bankei had led a hard life. In his youth he had questioned all the priests in the local temple and when they could not answer his questions satisfactorily he had stuffed his mouth with poisonous spiders in fury. He had spat them out before he was actually harmed but it set a precedent for the rest of his difficult life.

Though he was born on Buddha's birthday, 8 April 1622, Bankei spent much of his life as a Zen master railing against many of Zen's institutions such as koan practice, sutra chanting and even monasticism itself.

When he first embarked on the life of a Zen practitioner he led an extremely austere and even fanatical lifestyle. He walled himself up in a ten-foot cell, which had only one small opening, large enough for someone to extend an arm in to give him food twice a day. He mudded up the doorway so that no light could enter the cell.

He meditated by sitting upon a cold stone floor until his thighs and buttocks bled and became infected. He refused to eat any of the food passed to him and kept himself awake for days, splashing his face with cold water every time he became drowsy. Yet the enlightenment that he craved so seriously still eluded him.

He became sicker and sicker and spat up gobs of blood. Yet he was determined to either find the enlightenment he so desperately sought or die trying.

One day he felt a strong sensation in his throat and he spat out a huge ball of bloody phlegm. When it hit the wall in front of him and began to slide down, something about the movement of the phlegm and the colour of the blood released something in him and he attained a moment of realization. His realization that all things were already perfect in what he called the 'unborn' rocked him to his soul.

He immediately ate some rice and then broke out of his cell. When he went down to the creek to wash, the perfume of some nearby plum blossoms jolted him into yet another realization, connecting him deeply to what was 'unborn and undying'.

Later he became one of Zen's most famous and inspirational teachers. His message was simple: it is only by letting go of all intellectual and even religious ideas and instead abiding in our own original and unborn mind that true liberation is achieved. It is not through intellectual or religious practice, even Buddhist, that one can enter into the deep stream of enlightenment, but by being one's true self, without commentary, self-judgement or self-consciousness. It is everyday life that will lead the aspirant to the goal of self-realization, not chanting sutras or following religious dogma.

His message was not welcomed by the religious elite of his time, but had a deep effect on his many followers and listeners. Not only monks and nuns came to hear him speak, but farmers, fisherman, lay practitioners and housewives.

From having questioned all of his teachers as a young man and received unsatisfactory answers, his own understanding of the essence of Zen made him one of the most beloved figures of his time.

Blowing Out a Candle

The student came to the master one night and asked many questions. He was as full of questions as a melon is full of seeds. He kept asking them, one right after another, until late into the evening. It seemed that whenever the master answered one question there was another one waiting right behind it. The master could see that the student was trying to use his mind to understand dharma, which would get him nowhere.

Finally the student seemed to notice the late hour and got to his feet, apologizing to the master for keeping him so late. He went to the door of the master's room and looked out at the dark night. 'It is very dark out there,' he said, a little nervous at venturing out into the gloom.

The master rose and offered a lit candle to the student, who took it gratefully. But before he had gone out of the door the master quickly bent over and blew the candle out. The student stood for a moment, watching the wisps of smoke floating above the blackened wick of the candle. In that moment his mind was opened and he began to understand that all his questions had no purpose: that he himself was

the true question and by the act of blowing out the candle the master had illuminated his mind. He found he had no more questions that day, or any other after it, and was content to sit quietly and watch the world flow by like the flickering flame of a candle.

Blows Are Exchanged

When the famous Zen master Rinzai was a young student he was so shy that it took him three years to approach his master Obaku for a personal interview. One of the senior monks encouraged him to speak with the abbot.

Rinzai's reticence may not only have been down to his shyness but also to the fact that Obaku was known for his shouts, blows and disdain for traditional Buddhism. In any case, Rinzai entered the fierce abbot's quarters and asked him, 'What is the cardinal principle of Buddha dharma?', which was a stock phrase used in temples at that time. Obaku's answer was a blow that knocked the young novice to the floor.

Puzzled and dismayed, the young man went to the senior monk, whose name was Bokushu, and told him what had happened. Bokushu's advice was to try again. So the timid novice summoned the nerve to re-enter the abbot's quarters and repeated his questions. Once again he was knocked to the floor.

Rinzai went back to Bokushu and told him what had happened and the advice once more was to try again. So off to the abbot's quarters he went and repeated his question, only to receive yet another blow.

At this point Rinzai was convinced it was his fault he had received the blows. He obviously did not merit being a part of that community, so he resolved to leave the temple. Bokushu entreated him at least to pay his respects to Obaku before leaving.

Bokushu hurried to the abbot and told him about Rinzai's plan to leave, describing Rinzai as a very shy yet very talented young man. So when Rinzai went to say goodbye to Obaku, the abbot casually mentioned a fellow master named Daigu, who had a hermitage nearby, and suggested that Rinzai go there with his question.

Rinzai dutifully went off to Daigu's hermitage and explained to the old man what had happened with Obaku. But the old hermit reproved him, saying, 'Oh, so you didn't appreciate Obaku's grandmotherly kindness?'

For some reason this abruptly cleared Rinzai's mind and he shouted, 'Well, I guess there's not much to Obaku's dharma at all!' Daigu dealt him a blow in response, much as Rinzai's former master had done. But this time Rinzai gave him a blow in kind!

At this Daigu sent him off with the words, 'You're Obaku's problem, not mine. Go back to him!'

When Rinzai arrived back at Obaku's temple he was greeted by the abbot, who could easily see Rinzai's *satori* and shouted, 'So you've come back to pull the tiger's whiskers.' Rinzai replied with a loud *katsu* (shout) and Obaku laughingly told his attendant monk to take Rinzai back to the monk's quarters.

Years later Rinzai was hoeing in a field when Obaku came up to him. Rinzai immediately stopped what he was doing and leaned on his hoe.

'What,' said Obaku, 'tired already?'

'How can I be tired if I haven't picked up my hoe yet?' was Rinzai's reply.

At this, Obaku gave Rinzai one of his famous blows, but Rinzai snatched Obaku's walking stick and whacked him with it, knocking him to the ground.

Obaku got up, laughing, and bowed to his student.

Bodhidharma Comes
to the West

Bodhidharma, known as Dao Mo in China, was a realized sage from India. He arrived in China when he was around 64 years old. His meditation method was simple but powerful and is one of the most important roots of Chan (Zen) Buddhism. His manner was direct and simple.

Soon after his arrival in China, the emperor Wu heard of this powerful teacher and invited him to the royal court. Bodhidharma strode up to where the emperor was sitting on his throne and merely bowed his head instead of making the full prostrations the emperor's subjects usually offered.

The emperor was offended but he considered that this Bodhidharma was a barbarian from the western lands and probably did not know court etiquette. Besides, the emperor was interested in gleaning what knowledge this strange teacher, with his long hair and great bushy eyebrows, had to share with him.

Emperor Wu had been a great patron of Buddhism. True, he did not have the time or the inclination to do deep practices himself but he had built many temples in which he had sponsored numerous great religious ceremonies. He told all of this to Bodhidharma, elucidating the considerable merit he accrued from such pious acts, and expecting an impressed response from this new teacher, but Bodhidharma just stood there in silence. Not only that but he seemed to be positively glowering at the emperor underneath those great bushy eyebrows.

'What, in your opinion,' asked the emperor, 'is the value of my many meritorious acts?'

'None,' was the reply.

A bit disturbed at this, the emperor went on to question Bodhidharma. 'What would you say', he asked, 'is the basic teaching of Buddhism?'

Bodhidharma answered, 'Vast Emptiness'.

Emperor Wu waited to hear more but when he realized that Bodhidharma had nothing more to say, nothing more to share about the great subject of Buddhism, concerning which the emperor fancied himself an expert, he lost his temper and shouted at Bodhidharma, 'Just who do you think you are?'

At this, Bodhidharma answered simply, 'I don't know.' He then turned his back on the emperor and strode from the room. The emperor was furious and thought about having this rude and strange person beheaded immediately but decided it would gain him more merit to let him go.

Not finding any students of the Buddha whom he considered worthy of his teaching, Bodhidharma went to a cave in southern China and is said to have sat in a cave, facing a wall, meditating, for the next nine years.

Later he went out and taught, and is credited with creating what we now know as Chan or Zen Buddhism.

Burning the Buddha

It was cold, colder than it had been in some time, and the monks in the mountain temple were freezing. No matter how many robes they wore the meditation hall was still so cold they could barely keep still.

Outside, the snow had piled up so high the coal merchants were unable to deliver fresh supplies, and the little they'd had had been burned the day before. They could not even cook their rice, as there was no fuel for the cooks to boil water.

Imagine the monks' surprise when the master, Dan Xia, came into the meditation hall and began to remove the wooden statues of the Buddha from the altar, carrying them over to the brazier and setting them on fire.

While the warmth of the burning Buddhas was welcome, the fact that the master was burning the sacred statues upset all the monks. 'What are you doing?' they cried, unmindful of the status of their master. 'You are burning the sacred statues of the Buddha. How dare you insult the Buddha in this way?'

Master Dan Xia glared at them through the flames of the burning Buddhas. 'Are these statues alive?' he asked them. 'Do they have Buddha nature?'

'Well, no,' answered the monks, 'they are made from wood. How can they have Buddha nature?'

'Alright then,' said Dan Xia, 'they are just made of wood and can be used for fuel in an emergency situation such as this. They can be seen simply as firewood in this moment.'

The monks were all quiet then and moved closer to the burning Buddhas, which, as they were very old and made of an extremely hard wood, gave off much heat.

A few days later the weather changed, the snow began to melt and Dan Xia went into town and brought back new wooden Buddha statues. He set them on the altar and bowed to them and burned incense in front of them.

'Wait,' cried one of the monks, 'did you not say that the statues were just firewood and did not have Buddha nature? Are you worshipping firewood?'

'No,' answered Dan Xia, 'I am not worshipping firewood but honouring the Buddha that is represented by these statues.'

Complaining

The mountain temple was very far away from any towns and was famous for the strictness of its teachers. The master there believed that too much talking was a waste of energy and that complete silence allowed the monks to enter into the stillness of real Zen.

For this reason each monk who arrived at the temple was forced to follow a rule of silence. Not only did the monks meditate and eat in silence, as in other temples, but they also had to observe a strict code of silence in all of their work, study and even free time. Many found this rule too difficult to maintain and so left after a short time. But some welcomed the practice and enjoyed the vast emptiness that the silence opened up to them.

There was one exception to the silence rule. After ten years any monk who wished to could come before the master and speak, but just two words.

One monk, after being there the requisite time, came before the master. 'Well,' said the master, 'you have been here for ten years now. What two words do you wish to say?'

The monk looked at him and said, 'Hard . . . hard.' Then he turned and left the room.

Ten years later the same monk was called upon to speak his two words. 'Food . . . terrible,' he said, and again left the room.

After ten more long years had passed the monk once again was called into the master's room to speak his two words. He stood for some time in silence, the only sound in the room the deep and slow breathing of the master. Finally, the monk spoke up. 'I quit,' he said.

'Well,' said the master, 'I'm not surprised. All you do is complain!'

Throwing the Circle

Master Dasui was sitting in his quarters, drinking tea and thinking about nothing in particular, when there was a knock on his door. He sighed and put down his teacup. He so loved his quiet moments with just him and his tea. To be able to sit and sip in silence was one of his great joys.

To Master Dasui the spirit of tea was not unlike the spirit of Zen itself. To paraphrase the *Heart Sutra*, as he was fond of doing: 'Tea is not different from Zen, Zen not different from Tea.'

One of his teachers had famously said, 'To know the taste of tea is to know the taste of Zen.' Dasui agreed wholeheartedly. To sit in silence, to taste, with one's whole being, the deep richness of the powdered green tea, away from the hustle and bustle of the temple and all its duties, was a form of paradise for him.

But the knock on the door came again, low yet insistent. He put his cup down with a sigh and opened the door. One of the student monks was there. He bowed low and said, 'Master, there is a monk at the gate demanding to be let in.'

'What is his name?' asked Dasui.

'He will not tell us,' said the student monk, bowing even lower.

Dasui frowned; it was probably some renegade or, even worse, a disgraced monk. It was unheard of for a monk to demand anything, especially without providing his name and that of the temple in which he had trained. Dasui decided to go himself, see who this rude monk was and send him quickly on his way.

The master put down his cup and went outside, where a large monk with a fat belly was standing. The master looked him up and down and thought, 'I interrupted my tea time for this?'

The nameless monk just stood there, looking at him with an insolent and gruff expression. How rude, the master thought, and strode over to where the visitor stood.

He asked what the monk wanted. The monk stood there, without saying anything and looking stupid. The master turned to go back to his room and his pot of hot tea.

Suddenly the strange monk drew a large circle in the air and then made a motion of throwing it behind him. Then he bowed. The master turned to his student and said, 'Invite this wise monk in for tea.'

Dropping the Subject

Two monks were walking along when they came to a fast-running creek. They saw a woman there. She was obviously from high society and was dressed in silks. Yet she also had the air of a woman of 'the floating world' (a prostitute). When she saw the monks she beseeched them to carry her across the creek. Of course the monks had taken a vow not to have anything to do with the opposite sex. Imagine the surprise of one of the monks, then, when the other squatted down without a word and allowed the woman to climb onto his back. He then calmly carried her across the creek and set her down gently on the other side.

The other monk could not believe that his fellow monk had broken his vow so easily. As they walked along he fumed and fretted, and finally blurted out, 'I can't believe you just carried that woman, obviously of ill repute, across the creek like that! Did you forget your vows?'

The monk turned to him and said, 'Brother, I put the woman down and left her on the other side of the creek. But it seems that you are still carrying her!'

Even the Moon

Master Ryokan was sitting in his small meditation hut, marvelling at the full moon. Its light streamed through the window, illuminating the whole room with a soft light. He felt it enter his *hara*, in his lower abdomen, and warm his whole being.

Suddenly a thief entered the tiny space, intent on robbery. But when the thief looked around the room he saw nothing there that was worth stealing. Ryokan was very poor and owned very little. He most enjoyed sitting here under the moonlight and thinking about the Way. He ate only once a day and counted his students and his friends as his greatest gifts. He had no need for any others.

The thief went to leave the meditation hut but then Master Ryokan suddenly stirred. Looking at the thief, who was very ragged and thin, he said, 'I am so sorry that I have nothing of value for you to take. Please take my robe.'

And he removed his robe and handed it over to the thief, who, with a look of great surprise and delight, hurriedly went his way.

Master Ryokan sat naked, looking up in adoration at the exquisite sight of the full moon hanging over his hut. 'I wish,' he said to himself, 'that I could give the poor man this wonderful moon.'

Everything Annihilated

A young and very studious monk asked Master Dasui, 'At the end of this era when the fires burn everything up, will we be annihilated or not?'

'Annihilated all,' came the reply.

'Then we are annihilated along with everything else?' asked the monk.

'Along with everything else,' said Dasui.

Yet the young and studious (and very serious) monk could not accept that answer. It must be that the master is wrong, he said to himself. How could we, who are eternal in our Buddha nature, burn along with the fires of annihilation?

He was so disturbed that he left the temple and went to another temple and spoke to the master there, Master Datong, and told him of his discussion with Dasui.

Master Datong said nothing at first. He lit some sticks of incense before the statue of the Buddha and said, 'The great Buddha of the western river has arrived.' Then he turned to the young man and said, 'You must return to Master Dasui and atone for your great mistake.'

Shaken, the young monk immediately went back to his own temple but found upon arriving there that Dasui had died in his absence. Now really shaken, the young monk travelled back to Master Datong's temple only to find that he too had passed away.

The young monk went back to his own temple and gave himself over to serious contemplation of the causes of this annihilation and eventually found within himself a place of no being, no annihilation and no self. In other words, he attained the Way and no longer concerned himself with annihilation.

Facing a Wall

The master asked one day, 'What is the meaning of Bodhidharma facing a wall?'

One student answered, 'To show his deep connection to emptiness.'

'No,' said the master. 'That's not it.'

'It was to show he had no ties to the world of cause and effect,' said another.

'No,' said the master. 'That's not it either.'

The third student covered his ears.

'Yes,' said the master, 'that's just it.'

From Thief to Disciple

One quiet evening, as Master Kojun was sitting deep in meditation, a thief climbed through the open window. He crept into the room where Master Kojun was sitting and stopped at the doorway, expecting Master Kojun to jump up at the sound of his entrance. But Master Kojun just kept on sitting there, still and solid like a rock.

The thief looked around the room for something to steal, all the while keeping his eyes on the still form of Master Kojun. But the more he looked around the room, the more he could see it was just a simple room with no furniture to speak of, just a thin mat on the floor for sleeping and a small altar, in front of which Master Kojun sat. There was not even a statue on the altar that might be worth something to the thief. There was just a small sake jar with one flower in it.

He turned to leave the way he had come but Master Kojun spoke up. 'There is some money in that box in the corner,' he said. The thief went over to the box and took up the money.

'But leave me a little to pay the tax collector tomorrow,' said Master Kojun. There was something about his voice, deep and resonant yet not at all frightened, that made the thief feel he had no choice but to do what the strange monk said. He put a little of the money back into the box and turned once more to leave.

Master Kojun again spoke up. 'You should thank a person when you receive a gift,' he said, rather sternly.

The thief mumbled his thanks and climbed back out of the window.

The next day the thief was brought in front of Master Kojun, who was sat in the temple, ready to give a dharma talk. The policeman threw the ragged thief down in front of Master Kojun and said, 'This thief admits to robbing you last night.'

Master Kojun looked at the frightened thief and said, 'No, I do not think this man is a thief. He did come to me last night, needing money. I gave him some and he thanked me. That does not sound like a thief to me.'

The policeman had to let the thief go and turned away in disgust. The thief crawled over to Master Kojun and prostrated himself before him. Master Kojun then asked some of his students to take the poor man and feed him and give him new clothing.

The thief was so touched by the warm heart of Master Kojun that he asked to stay at the temple and in time he become one of Master Kojun's best disciples.

Fuke's Bell

Fuke was the quintessential 'holy fool'. He used to wander about the town ringing a bell and shouting, 'What comes in brightness I ring in brightness. What comes in darkness I ring in darkness. If it comes from all directions I dance through it like a whirlwind.'

His friend and fellow Zen master Rinzai sent one of his students to grab hold of Fuke and bring him to the temple but Fuke wriggled out of the student's grasp like an eel.

Another time Fuke went about the town begging everyone for a robe. His own was in tatters and it appeared as though he wanted to upgrade his image. But for some reason no one was moved to give him one.

When Rinzai heard about this he sent one of his students with a coffin telling him that he had made him a robe.

Fuke grabbed up the coffin and hoisted it upon his shoulders with great glee, calling out, 'My good friend Rinzai has made me this beautiful robe. I will now go to the east gate of the city to die!'

A bunch of onlookers followed him to the east gate while he pranced and danced through the streets carrying his 'robe'. But when they got there Fuke seemed to change his mind and said, 'I think today is not the day for me to die. Instead I will go to the south gate of the city tomorrow and die there.'

The next day he did much the same thing, assuring everyone at the south gate that he would go to the west gate on the following day and die there. Once again, though, he did not do it, and the people gave up on him, such that when he went to the north gate of the city the next day no one followed him. But there he laid himself down in his coffin, calling out to a passer-by to nail on the lid.

When the passer-by went to the market and reported what had happened, everyone rushed over to the north gate to find Fuke's coffin there, with the lid nailed down. They stood for quite a while, not knowing what to do. Should they believe that the trickster Fuke was in the coffin or not? Finally they decided to open the coffin, only to find it empty except for Fuke's little bell. And it seemed to many of them that they could hear the sound of the bell ringing somewhere in the air above them.

Great Waves

There was once a sumo wrestler named Onami, 'Great Waves'. He was immensely strong and could beat anyone at his school, even his teacher. But when he had to wrestle in public he became so nervous that even weaker men could easily defeat him.

Finally, not being able to bear it any longer, Onami decided that what he needed to do was go and see a Zen master for help. It so happened that a wandering Zen master named Hakuju was staying at a temple near the sumo school. So Onami went there and told the teacher of his problem.

'Your name is Great Waves, yet you do not experience yourself this way,' said Master Hakuju. 'Stay here in the temple tonight and meditate upon yourself as huge waves, sweeping everything before you. If you are successful at this you will be unbeatable.'

So Onami sat throughout the night, trying to see himself as a great wave, washing everything before it. At first it was very difficult but after a long time of perseverance he was able to feel himself as a great wave, stronger and vaster than anything else. The waves grew bigger and bigger, washing away the altar in front of which he was sitting. Then they washed away the very temple in which he sat. The whole world was one great wave, rushing back and forth. By morning the waves had calmed down and the entire world was a vast sea, still and silent.

When Master Hakuju came back in the morning he found Onami sitting in meditation, with a small smile upon his great round face. He patted him gently upon his giant shoulder and said, 'Now there is nothing that will disturb you. Remember, you are those waves, washing everything before you.'

The next day Onami entered a sumo contest. This time, instead of being too nervous to wrestle, he saw himself as the great waves of the sea and swept all opponents before him. From this time on, Onami was unbeatable.

Hakuin and the
Old Man of Shoju

When the great Zen master Hakuin was young and full of himself he went to visit a famous hermit teacher named Dokyo, also called the Old Man of Shoju, who lived high in a mountain hermitage.

When he first met Master Dokyo, Hakuin, named Ekaku at the time, boasted of his knowledge and deep understanding of Zen. He had written a poem about his realization in fine calligraphy on a piece of expensive paper. This he extended towards Dokyo with a little bow.

Dokyo snatched up the paper and, to Ekaku's great surprise and consternation, crushed it in his left hand. He then held his right hand out to the young man and demanded, 'Other than intellectual knowledge what have you really experienced?'

Not to be outdone by the eccentric hermit, Ekaku answered, 'If I had really experienced something, surely I would now show it to you. I'd vomit it out,' he said, and made some rude gagging noises over Dokyo's outstretched hand.

Dokyo smiled and moved closer to Ekaku. 'How then do you explain Joshu's *mu*?'

Here Dokyo was referring to a famous story of the great Zen master Joshu who, upon being asked by one of his students if a dog has Buddha nature, answered *mu* or no. This later became one of the more famous koans or Zen riddles, which students were required to struggle through to show they understood what Joshu meant with his enigmatic reply.

For instance, was he actually saying that dogs have no Buddha nature when it is well accepted in Buddhist doctrine that all living things have Buddha nature? Or was his reply of *mu* (*wu* in Chinese) really meant to represent the negation of outer form of intellectual understanding of Zen as opposed to 'belly' or '*hara*' understanding?

Mu can mean 'no' or it can mean something like no thing or no thought. Joshu's *mu* koan is usually the first one that Zen students are given. They are required to sit with this koan and come up with an answer, using not their intellectual mind but their 'Buddha mind' or 'true mind'. Since this is not merely an exercise in inductive reasoning, or any kind of 'reasoning', the koan forces the student to make a leap beyond reason to arrive at an answer that applies to them personally or to their own understanding.

By questioning Ekaku concerning a 'kindergarten' level of koan, Dokyo was making a statement about just how high he thought Ekaku's attainment really was.

Of course Ekaku had already spent many hours wrestling with this koan. When other young monks had slackened off their practice to rest or enjoy the day Ekaku had refused to join them, instead remaining in deep meditation on the koan. Even when there had been an earthquake and everyone else had run out of the temple, Ekaku remained sitting calmly on his cushion, seeking to unlock the riddle of Joshu's *mu*.

He'd remained there, scarcely stopping for food and sleep, but one day had been overcome by what he called a great sense of doubt. All sense of himself as a young student monk had gone and all that remained in his consciousness was '*mu*'. It was as though he were encased in a great sheet of ice. He could not move forward or backwards but was frozen in place, in *mu*.

Then, a few days later, the sound of the temple bell had brought him out of his entrapment and he returned to his senses. All of his doubts disappeared and he felt that at last he understood what *mu* really was. There really was no path to enlightenment, there were no cycles of birth and death to escape, and there was nothing to which he needed to aspire.

Of course, as with many first *kensho* or realization experiences, his was only a partial understanding, but the young monk felt that he stood on the precipice of something very special and grand, and it was with this attitude that he had approached the old hermit.

Now, looking at the old master's outstretched hand, he replied, 'In Joshu's *mu* there is no place for hands or feet', thus ridiculing the old man's gesture.

Of course Dokyo was not cowed by this. Instead he suddenly reached out and gave Ekaku's nose a painful twist. 'Aha,' he said, 'I have found some place for hands and feet.'

At this Ekaku admitted defeat and, prostrating himself at Dokyo's feet, he begged to become his student.

Ekaku studied with the Old Man of Shoju for some time. He returned to his extreme, ascetic practices of denying himself food or sleep in his mighty quest for true understanding, while Dokyo constantly ridiculed him.

One day – a rare occasion when he had actually taken time off from his meditation to go into the nearby village to beg – he ran into a local character who, for some reason, hated begging monks. The ruffian knocked Ekaku to the ground with a club, knocking him out.

Interestingly, once he regained consciousness everything that he had been spending so much painful time on suddenly became very clear to him. This time it was indeed not a 'mind' understanding but a 'belly' understanding.

Ekaku got up and began dancing along the street, overcome with joy. The villagers decided that the knock on the head had destroyed his wits and shrank back from the dancing, laughing figure.

When Ekaku returned to Dokyo's hermitage the old master could see at once that his student had indeed penetrated into a deeper level of understanding. After asking him a few testing questions Dokyo clapped his student on the back and congratulated him. Then he told him to quit his ascetic practice and now spend some time in restoring his health.

His Cup Runneth Over

There was once a great student of Zen. He had studied with all the masters he could find, had logged countless hours of *zazen* and had experienced numerous instances of *satori*, or insight. His goal was to become the greatest Zen master of all time. He had numerous students, who all clamoured to be his number one. He built the largest temple anyone had ever seen and every day it was filled with students, monks, scholars and lay people. They burned incense, chanted the sutras and sat *zazen* deep into the night. He wore costly robes of silk, imported from China, and drank his tea out of the finest, most delicate porcelain, also from China. His dharma talks were always full and everyone looked up to him as a true Zen master. Yet he was not happy.

He had a feeling that he was missing something important about Zen that he could not put his finger on. Even though he knew he was progressing well, he still felt a long way from complete realization. Every time he heard of a new master he would hurry to meet him and see if there was anything he could glean from him.

One day he heard of an old master living on the outskirts of town who was said to have attained sagehood. Curious, he slipped out of his busy temple and, leaving his usual retinue behind, went to see this old master.

He was very surprised to find the old man living in a quite dilapidated building out on the far end of town, almost into the forest. At first he was sure he had come to the wrong place. The building was so old and worn he could not imagine anyone living in it. The boards on the walls were all warped and devoid of paint. The straw on the roof was threadbare and didn't look like it could possibly keep the rain out.

He went up to the door and hesitantly knocked. 'Come in,' rang out a strong voice from within. Intrigued, he slid the door open and looked inside. There was an old, old man, sitting upright and looking straight at him. He bowed, removed his sandals and entered the building. Seating himself opposite the old man, he bowed again and introduced himself.

'Ah,' said the old man, 'I have heard of you.'

At this he felt happy. It seemed his great reputation had already travelled this far. He began to list his many accomplishments and spiritual insights. He went on for some time, the old master remaining silent all the way through. When, at last, he was done, the old master said nothing for a time. Then he suddenly spoke up.

'Would you like some tea?' he asked.

Without waiting for an answer the old master went over to a kettle that had been bubbling away behind them the whole time and filled an ancient teapot. Then he got out the powdered tea and gently poured some into the hot water. He took up a tea whisk, as ancient as the teapot, and stirred the tea briskly for a moment or so. Then he brought the teapot and two small cups over to where they had been talking.

The Zen student noticed that the cups were made of *raku* pottery, and were roughly glazed, with uneven edges. 'Just so,' he thought. 'Of course the old master would be a follower of Rikyu, the originator of this style of simple pottery.' He was all set to tell the old master everything he knew of Rikyu, but the master held one hand up, palm towards the Zen student. Then he began to pour tea into the cup in front of his visitor.

He poured, very slowly and gently, but instead of stopping when the tea reached the brim of the cup, he kept on pouring until the scalding liquid ran over the top of the cup and onto the table, then onto the lap of his visitor. The Zen student leaped up as the hot liquid spilled on him, burning his thighs. 'What are you doing?' he cried out, forgetting his manners completely.

The old master looked at him and smiled gently. 'You have studied a long time and have acquired a great deal of knowledge,' he said, 'and that is good, but . . .' – and here he looked at his guest with a sad look on his old, lined face – 'I'm afraid that, like this cup, your mind and heart are already too full to be able to take any of my teachings. My friend, you will need to empty your cup before it can be filled again.'

It is said that the Zen student dropped everything then and there, and became the student of the old master. He gave up all of his titles, his fancy robes, the great temple he had built, even all of his students, and instead lived out the rest of his days drinking tea and talking happily with the old master until the day he died. He gave up all his yearnings and attempts to reach enlightenment and just enjoyed each day, one moment at a time.

His Wisdom Eye

The student came to the master and told him that the spring from which their community received their water had been plugged up by sand.

He bowed and waited to receive his orders. The master said nothing. The student bowed once more and turned to leave the room. Suddenly the master said, 'If the spring is obstructed by sand, what is your wisdom eye obstructed by?'

The student did not know what to say. He only worked in the grounds and, unlike the other students, never sat in meditation – nor could he read the sacred texts. He waited to hear the answer, hoping he would understand it when it came.

'Your wisdom eye', said the master, 'is obstructed by your eye.'

At this the student turned to go, shaking his head. When he heard a chuckle behind him he turned towards the master, who gave him a wide smile and nodded to him. At this the student's wisdom eye opened all at once and he fell to his knees in gratitude.

How Sweet It Is

A monk was going along, humming a little song to himself, enjoying the bright summer day, when a tiger suddenly appeared and began to chase him. The monk ran as fast as he could, but the tiger was faster and was gaining on him quickly.

The monk ran so fast that he did not look where he was going and suddenly he ran right off the edge of a cliff. Fortunately, there was a thick vine growing right below the precipice and the monk grabbed onto it for dear life.

The tiger ran to the edge of the cliff, looked down at the monk and roared a great horrible roar, which froze the breath of the poor man. But he clung onto the vine with all his strength. Then, to his horror, he heard the roar of another tiger! Only this one was coming from the bottom of the cliff. Looking down, he saw another tiger waiting below to gobble him up the minute he let go of the vine.

There he hung, between two tigers, his whole body trembling with fear. To his further horror, he saw two mice, one white and one black, gnawing on the life-saving vine. He felt it begin to give way under his weight and he knew he did not have long to live.

Suddenly he noticed a wild strawberry plant growing out of the cliff edge. Without even thinking about it he reached out and picked one. He placed it into this mouth and exclaimed, 'Oh, how sweet it is!'

How to Speak

The student went to ask the master some questions about the path of Zen but before he could get a word out, the master told him not to speak.

'Why can't I speak?' asked the student.

The master replied, 'First, close your mouth. Only then will you be able to speak.'

Hui Neng, the Illiterate Master

Hui Neng worked in the monastery kitchen and was looked down upon by the other monks as being an illiterate rustic. When it came time for the Fifth Patriarch, Hung Jen, to pass on his mantle, he decided to hold a poetry contest to come up with his successor. So he gathered his students together and gave them instructions on writing a poem describing the experience of enlightenment.

Shen Xiu, his senior student, duly wrote a poem on the wall of the corridor that led into the meditation hall. He wrote:

> Our body is the bodhi tree
>
> and our mind a mirror bright.
>
> Carefully we wipe them hour by hour
>
> and let no dust alight.

This impressed all the other students and it seemed as though Shen Xiu had a lock on the contest but Hung Jen was not so sure. Hui Neng, busy in the kitchen and serving the other monks their meals, heard their excited conversation about Shen Xiu's poem. One night he had a sudden experience of illumination and came up with a poem of his own. Of course he could not write it out himself, being illiterate, but he got one of the younger monks to write it out for him. His went like this:

> There is no bodhi tree
>
> Nor stand of a mirror bright.
>
> Since all is void,
>
> where can dust alight?

When the Fifth Patriarch came upon this poem he realized that Hui Neng was the one he had been looking for.

So, under the cover of nightfall, Hung Jen gave Hui Neng the title of the Dharma of Sudden Enlightenment and the robe of office and sent him out on his own, to keep him safe from the angry monks, who were outraged at his choice of successor.

Laer, Hui Neng went on to build what is now called the Southern School of Chan Buddhism.

The Flower Sermon

It was early evening and the Buddha's followers were gathering up on Vulture Peak for his nightly sermon. Many people in his community had gathered there, including monks, householders and even nobles. There was an air of expectancy and excitement as everyone found places to sit and await the wise words of the Awakened One.

In the front row sat some of his most trusted and experienced followers, including his cousin, Mahakasyapa, who had followed him for years now. In the years since his enlightenment experience under the bodhi tree it often seemed to the Buddha that he had walked over the entire land of India. But while his body felt exhausted his spirit remained strong. His mind was still clear and his will indomitable.

The problem was putting his experiences and insights into words that his followers could understand and apply to their own lives. In his experience, true understanding was something that was beyond words. No matter how many times he tried to describe his awakening and the knowledge that he had gained in that instant, he found himself wrestling with concepts and images that he could barely describe.

He was not interested in offering abstract ideas to his students. He wanted to be of use, to offer them something that would make their often-challenging lives if not easier, at least more rewarding. He

had tried many ways of using words to help them but he felt that whatever words or images he used he was missing out something of vast importance.

Once again, his followers and students, the learned and the illiterate, had gathered this evening. They were waiting for the Buddha to fill them with his wisdom, to lighten their spiritual load, to inspire and uplift them. The low hum of hundreds of voices filled the evening air, drowning out the usual insect serenade.

Finally the Buddha made his way slowly through the crowd and up to his usual place on a low rock overhang. They waited to hear his deep voice, which always carried easily whenever he spoke, but on this night he was silent for so long that his students and then the crowd at the back began to whisper among themselves, wondering when their revered teacher would begin speaking.

Longer and longer he sat there, looking out over the throng with a small smile on his lips, his breathing deep and steady. Then, when the tension had built to an almost unbearable crescendo, he suddenly lifted his right arm and raised it to the level of his head, still without speaking. In his hand he held a lotus flower.

The whispering stopped for a moment, then restarted as everyone waited for him to begin. Why was he not speaking? they asked each other. Was he perhaps ill or had he run out of things to teach them?

As he sat in silence, simply holding up the flower, some people at the back began to rise and take their leave, convinced there would be no teaching that night.

Yet Mahakasyapa, who had followed him for many seasons now as they made their way across India, found himself smiling back at his teacher. There was something just so perfect about the Buddha sitting in silence and simply holding out this lotus flower, a symbol of spiritual purity, that filled him with joy and gratitude. He could not help smiling a great wide smile.

The Buddha took one last look around and then nodded to Mahakasyapa, whom he later made his first successor, as it was he and only he who understood the Flower Sermon.

And thus, say the stories, Zen was born.

Killing the Buddha

Master Linji was known as a fierce Zen master, even among fierce Zen masters. He taught that the only way to enlightenment was total commitment to the Way. One had to live every moment as if it were the last moment. This approach to practice was a big influence not only on Zen practitioners but also on the samurai, who, upon going into battle, used this philosophy.

Master Linji is often quoted as saying, 'Get rid of anything that stands in the way of your cultivation. Even if you come upon the Buddha on your path do not let him distract you for a moment. If you should meet the Buddha in this way you must kill him!

'And if you should meet the patriarchs on your road, kill them as well. Even if you should meet with *arhats* (saints) on your path, kill them as well!'

Leaving the Leaves

The young acolyte had been working for the tea master for only a short time. He had watched as the tea master served his many and often famous guests, nobles from the capital and such like, though he had never actually *seen* him serve the noble guests. He had never been invited to enter the austere tea hut where the *chanoyu* ceremony took place.

It was his job to make sure everything outside the tea hut was in perfect order for the noble guests. He, of course, never spoke to any of them, nor did they ever speak to him. Instead, he would stand in a deep bow as they passed through the gate to the tea garden. He watched, as well as he could, from his deep bow, as they made their way down the stone-mapped pathway to the tea hut itself, which stood at the back of the garden.

Of course the tea master would have already met them at the gate, the one that separated the outer garden and the inner garden, where the tea hut itself stood. The tea master always made sure he bowed a little deeper, a little lower than did his illustrious guests. They would then walk the short way down the stone-studded path, all the while admiring the small but shapely trees and bushes that lined it, the pine, cedar and oak trees that were maintained scrupulously by the gardener, another old and tight-lipped man.

All the while the acolyte would be standing there, still and bowed down like the limbs of the small pine trees that lined the path. (Not that the noble guests ever noticed him. Their eyes would glide over him as if he were just another tree limb, though not as artistic and aesthetic as the tree limbs themselves.)

Then, outside the tea hut, they would pause at an ancient stone water basin, there to rinse out their mouths and wash their hands in order to purify themselves before entering the sacred space of the tea hut.

Of course, they would be forced not only to remove their swords if they were samurai, but also to get down on their hands and knees in order to enter the tea hut through its very small and extremely low doorway. The acolyte always enjoyed the sight of these demure and noble beings waving their bottoms in the air as they entered the tea hut. Oftentimes he would snicker to himself at the sight of such haughty noblemen being forced to humble themselves in this way.

(He would be careful, though, not to make any actual noise at these times, especially when it was a fierce samurai who was crawling on his hands and knees like an infant. After all, the samurai had the power of life and death over a commoner such as himself. Some of them were happy to lop the head off any common person who merely irritated, never mind actually insulted, them.)

He would remain standing there, head bowed down, eyes turned to the ground at his feet, until the tea ceremony was finished and the guests had left the tea garden, though it was often very boring and sometimes even painful to do so.

As sweeper in the tea garden, it was his job to maintain the purity and cleanliness of the stone path. These stones were laid out in precise patterns, as described by the great tea master Rikyu. There had to be a graceful balance between *watari*, or practicality, and *kei*, or artistic balance. The stones had to be slightly off-centre to each other and large enough that visitors could put an entire foot on each stone.

The stones themselves were set into the ground and had been brought from riverbeds or even the sea, often a considerable distance away. It was his job, as sweeper, to ensure there was never any chance of a guest slipping on an over-wet one and falling on his noble behind.

It was also his job to make sure there were no leaves or twigs or, Buddha forbid, any dirt on these immaculate stepping-stones. He spent many long hours picking up tiny twigs and small stones with his

bare hands, bent over like a *bonsai* tree.

The leaves were the main problem. Not matter how many times he swept the stones free of them, they would inevitably waft down from the surrounding trees and paper the ground before him. Many of them were too delicate to sweep away and he had to get down on hands and knees, like a noble guest, to pick them up one by one.

One day, as they were preparing to receive some very high-level guests, the tea master came up behind him as he did his leaf picking and stood there silently while he removed every last leaf. He had spent a large part of an hour already on this onerous task and when he finally stood up straight, he had to rub his lower back before it would release.

The tea master stood there, as silent as a pine tree, looking up and down the path. The acolyte stood proudly, knowing that he had done a superior job of leaf picking. Then the tea master reached up to a branch slightly above his head and shook its leaves down upon the stone path.

The acolyte stood there, speechless, as the leaves wafted gently upon the path, like graceful *obon* dancers. Once they had finished their graceful glide, the tea master looked around him, turned to the acolyte and nodded, a small smile upon his lips, and then turned back to the outer gate to greet his guests.

Mind Waving

Two monks were standing under a pole from which hung a banner. The banner was waving in the breeze and the two monks were arguing about whether it was the breeze or the banner that was moving.

They had spent the whole morning arguing like this. These two monks loved nothing more than to have a good argument, so much so that the other monks would walk if not run when they saw them coming.

Like hopeless gamblers, they would find the most ridiculous things to argue about: for example, whether the sun was shining through the clouds or the clouds through the sun; whether a dog, or perhaps a tree, has Buddha nature; even whether the Buddha had been a real person.

They argued over whether it was better to be silent in their practice or to read the sutras aloud. They argued over whether their teacher, Hui Neng, was actually enlightened or not, or whether any of the other monks in the temple had reached enlightenment. They argued over the koan, 'What is the sound of one hand?' and what that really means. They argued about whether the day was to be a good or bad one. They even argued over whether bugs had Buddha nature, asking what that actually meant for them if they did.

Throughout the morning they had stood beneath the banner, gently blowing in the breeze, and all the other monks have given them a wide berth, afraid of being drawn into the argument, as so often happened.

Master Hui Neng watched them yelling back and forth, each sure that he was right. Finally, he could stand it no longer and went out to where they stood, looking up at the banner. 'Master,' they said, 'please tell us the truth. Is it the banner that is moving or is it the wind?'

Hui Neng looked up at the banner once more and turned to the two irascible monks. 'It is neither the wind nor the banner that is moving,' he told them, 'it is your mind.'

For once the two monks were speechless (though later that evening they were seen in the kitchen, arguing about how best to prepare tofu).

Nanquan Kills the Cat

For some reason the monks were arguing about a cat. It had been hanging around the monastery kitchen, hoping to snatch a bit of food after breakfast. It was quite a mangy cat. Its fur was matted and rough, one of its ears was gone and its ribs showed through its skin. Altogether it was a sorry sight.

One of the kitchen staff had spied it sneaking in, and had snatched it up and carried it out to the yard. The monks started arguing about whether the cat had Buddha nature. They were all familiar with the famous koan about whether a dog has Buddha nature but they were not sure about a cat.

Master Nanquan heard them and came out to see what was going on. Upon seeing the cat he immediately snatched it up and held it out to the monks. The cat meowed piteously, looking around at the monks as Master Nan held it tightly by the scruff of its neck. The younger monks began to feel pity for the poor creature. Perhaps they should just feed it a little and chase it away, a few of them mumbled. The truth was they were a bit afraid of Master Nan, who had a legendary temper.

Now he frowned at the young monks while he held the cat up. He disappeared for a moment into the kitchen and then came back out with a sharp cleaver. The cook came out behind him, rubbing his hands on his apron, clearly worried about the fate of his favourite cleaver.

The master glared fiercely at the monks while he held the sharp blade over the struggling cat. 'Whoever can say the right word about this cat will save it. Otherwise I will cut it in two.'

The monks looked at each other. What could they say? They wanted to save the cat but were afraid of saying the wrong thing to Master Nan. They were not sure if the dog koan applied here. They all held their tongues, sure that Master Nan would relent and let the cat go.

But to their surprise and dismay Master Nan raised the cleaver and quickly chopped the cat in half. He let both halves drop to the ground and looked around at the monks, as if daring one of them to speak up, but they all just looked at the ground, saying nothing, horrified and chagrined.

Later on, one of the senior students, Zhaozhou, came back to the temple from his travels and Master Nan told him about the incident with the cat. Zhaozhou looked at Master Nan for a moment and then, placing his sandals on his head, left the room.

Master Nan looked out the door as Zhaozhou, his sandals still on his head, left the temple. 'If you had been here,' called Master Nan to him, 'that cat would have been saved.'

No Working, No Eating

When the Zen master Hyakujo was in his eighties he would still do manual labour with his students. He loved especially to trim the broken branches from trees after a storm. He would set out at dawn, even before his students, and climb high into the trees to trim them.

His students constantly worried that he would fall out of a tree someday. He was so old they were sure his bones were quite brittle and would easily break in a fall. Not only that but he started working much earlier than them and quit much later.

Often, when he was high in a tree, he understood a little of what birds must feel, so far above the earth. In truth, he did not mind the prospect of falling from the sky and dying in this way, like an old or sick bird.

He also felt a great need to be useful. He did not consider his dharma talks to his students to be particularly valuable. He could see that for a third of the students his talk went completely over their heads; another third would be half or even completely asleep, and the other third would nod their heads as if they understood every word he said, even though he knew they did not.

So he loved working with his hands. He loved using tools, tools that he had made by his own hands. He loved interacting with nature. He loved planting something and watching it grow. He loved building things, fixing things and improving things.

But his students worried about him. Even if they could not understand everything he taught them, they did know that he was a holy man and special in the way that only very holy men and women are.

And he was old, older than anyone else at the temple, so, as well as fearing that he might fall out of a tree sometime, they were equally worried that he might drop one of the heavy building stones and injure himself.

So one day they hid his tools from him, in the hope that he would get the message and work less and meditate more. But instead he just sat in his room and, despite his students bringing him food three or more times a day, refused to eat a bite. This went on for some days and his students began to worry less about him falling from a tree and more about him starving to death.

So, finally, they relented and brought him his tools. He took them up gladly and said to them, 'No work, no eat.' Then he went out to the orchard. And thus did Master Hyakujo begin a tradition that was to endure in Zen temples from then on.

One-arm Zen

Huike had heard that there was a great master meditating in a cave outside of the village where he lived. In great excitement Huike ran up to the cave and peered inside. There at the back of the cave sat a great form, facing the wall and sitting so still he seemed to be made of stone himself. Huike noticed that the man had dark skin, like a foreigner's.

He shouted out to the man, saying, 'Great master, please forgive me for interrupting your meditation but I would like to become your student. I have long searched for a master to teach me the Way and I have been told that you are such a one.'

The man did not answer. He did not acknowledge Huike in any way. Thinking perhaps that the master had not heard him, Huike ventured a little way into the cave and asked again to be accepted as a student. The master still did not answer. He sat so still and unmoving it seemed he might be dead but Huike could see his belly rising and falling with his deep breathing. Surely, thought Huike to himself, this is a great master.

He stood there for some time, waiting until the master was finished with his mediation, but the whole afternoon went by and still the master did not move. Perhaps, thought Huike, I should come back in the morning before he begins his mediation tomorrow.

And so he went back to the village and told his fellow Zen students that he had found a great teacher and that he would soon be his student. His friends all congratulated him on his great good fortune and Huike could hardly sleep that night.

He was up very early the next morning and, after making up a little rice to offer the master, he placed it into a bowl and wrapped the bowl in a cloth. He practically ran all the way to the cave, only to find the master already in his mediation, still facing the back wall of the cave.

Not knowing what to do, he placed the bowl of rice in the doorway of the cave and then sat down himself, thinking to join the master in his meditation. But the morning hours went by very slowly and Huike became quite hungry. He thought it might be all right to have a little of the rice. After all, he had brought so much. So he ate a little rice, drank from the stream that ran near the cave, and then sat down again.

Huike had meditated for many years now, having been instructed in the art by a travelling holy man, but he found it very difficult. He just could not sit for any length of time without his knees and back hurting him. His mind often wandered too, and he became bored after a short while. Watching the foreign teacher sitting there so immobile, like a carved figure, he felt that he would learn so much from him.

But the teacher would not acknowledge him, no matter how long he stayed there waiting for him to finish his meditation. Finally Huike gave up and went back to the village. He told his friends that the master would not acknowledge him and that he was giving up, but they all said, 'No, no, he is just testing you. You must not give up so easily.'

So the next day he went there again and once more called out to the master, 'I am Huike and I wish to become your student. Please teach me', and then he bowed so low his forehead struck the dirt at his feet. But the master did not respond in any way, though Huike saw that the rice bowl was empty. Seeing this, he hurried back to the village and cooked up some more rice.

So began a series of days in which Huike waited at the cave opening for the master to give some sign that he had heard his earnest entreaties, but the master never moved. Each night Huike would tell his friends that he was giving up, that there was obviously something wrong with him or with the foreign teacher, but each time they told him not to give up, that the man was a great teacher from a faraway land called India, and that his name was Bodhidharma, which meant Penetrating Clarity.

He was a great master, they told him, and had reached complete enlightenment, and would lead Huike there as well provided he did not give up. They were simple farmers but they had grown up with Huike and knew that he had longed for a teacher for many years, so they encouraged him to be patient. One day the teacher will acknowledge you, they told him; just don't give up.

And so Huike waited patiently for the master to notice him, each day bringing him rice and sitting outside the cave. He sat there quietly, watching the master sitting himself so quietly and so solidly.

He began to try and follow the breathing of the master, but found that he needed to take three or four breaths for every one of the master's. But as he sat and tried to follow the master he found his ability to sit quietly in meditation was growing greater each day. His breathing slowed down, not as much as the master's but until he was breathing much slower than he had ever breathed before. His mind quietened sufficiently for hours to go by without him even noticing them. Only when the sun began to go down did he suddenly realize and jump up, bowing again at the cave entrance and running back to the village before it got too dark to see the path.

This went on for some time. Autumn flowed into winter and it began to get colder up there at the cave. Huike would put on his warmest robe but the cold still reached beneath it and pierced him. Bodhidharma, meanwhile, just sat as he had always sat, facing the wall and breathing slowly, like a mountain.

After spending so many days in this way, Huike felt his heart and spirit open, bit by bit, as if he were already being taught by the master. He began to notice little things in his environment that he had not noticed before, even though he had lived in this small village all his life. Suddenly the voices of the birds began to speak to him in a language that he could understand. Even the breeze in the trees began speaking to him in a voice that he heard and could make sense of, as if it, like him, were a person.

Sometimes the light that flowed into his eyes seemed to blind him, it was so bright. Other times he seemed to be able to see in the dark, so bright was it even then. He found himself moving so much more slowly than he had done previously, dancing gently like the trees that swayed in the breeze around him instead of running up and down the path to and from the cave.

He began to notice the people around him, as well, and how they often tried to hide what they really felt: how they put on a brave face when they were afraid, or how they smiled and laughed when they were actually crying inside. He found his understanding and love for his friends and fellow villagers growing day by day.

He felt that he was indeed close to understanding the world and his place within it in a way that he had never done before. He became convinced that with the right guidance from an enlightened teacher he himself might become an enlightened teacher in time.

But in all this time, the meditating master had never spoken to him or acknowledged him in any way. Huike sometimes grew angry at this and at other times became quite despondent.

Finally he decided that he would stay there at the cave until the master acknowledged him, no matter how long it took. So he sat there for days, not eating, not sleeping. When he became too sleepy to sit, he stood. At first he was very cold but after some time of deep and slow breathing (he could match the master much better now) he found a sense of warmth rising from deep within himself.

But the master never moved, never spoke or even seemed to see the world around him, so deep was his meditation.

The days got colder and snow began to fall. At first Huike was able to keep himself relatively warm but soon he began to feel like a frozen stick of wood. Why had the master never acknowledged him? Why, when Huike had been so steadfast and patient, had he never turned to speak to him? Why, when his visitor was so obviously dedicated to his practice, did he not welcome him as his student?

Huike stood there in the blinding snow and his mind began to race until he began to question his very existence. What good did it do him, he thought, to sit so patiently and meditate so deeply while the master just sat there and never even noticed him? He began to lose hope. Perhaps he was never meant to become an enlightened teacher, he thought; maybe he was just a blockhead, like a piece of firewood, only good for cooking rice.

He was thinking this way when he noticed an axe leaning up against a nearby tree. His first thought was how negligent it was for the woodcutter to leave his precious tool there in the snow. Then an idea began to form in his mind, and no matter how he tried to un-form it, it would not let go.

Finally he walked stiffly over to where the axe lay and brought it back to the cave entrance. Then, as if in a kind of trance, he laid his left arm on a large, somewhat flat rock there. He looked at it for some time, this arm that he had carried with him his whole long life. Suddenly he brought the axe up over his head and swung it down heavily, chopping off his arm in one blow.

At first he just sat there dumbly, watching the blood spurt out of the place where his arm had been, turning the snow around him a deep red. He knew he should feel great pain at this but for some reason he did not. He continued to watch the blow flow out spasmodically until suddenly it stopped.

He felt a hand on his upper arm, squeezing it tightly so that the blood ceased to flow. He looked up and saw the great piercing gaze of Bodhidharma looking down at him. He looked at him with such deep compassion that Huike wanted to bow down to the earth right away, but Bodhidharma held him up and, tearing a piece of cloth from his own robe, bound up Huike's arm.

Later Huike and Bodhidharma sat together in the cave. Bodhidharma sat facing Huike now, his back to the cave wall that he had gazed upon for so long. Huike sat, happy now that the great master had come to his aid. He felt a little foolish yet he also felt very relieved.

'What is it you want from me?' asked Bodhidharma, in a gentle yet fierce voice.

Huike immediately thought of so many things that he wanted to know and learn from this great teacher. But all he said was, 'My mind is so turbulent. Please pacify it.'

'Bring me this turbulent mind,' said Bodhidharma, 'and I will pacify it.'

Huike's thoughts began to race, as they so often did. 'But I don't know where this mind resides,' he said. 'I cannot bring it to you.'

'Then,' said Bodhidharma, 'I have already pacified it', and he had.

Huike remained with his teacher for many years and before Bodhidharma left to return to India he transmitted his Dharma Seal to Huike, who did indeed become a great teacher himself.

One-finger Zen

Whenever anyone asked Master Gutai about the true meaning of Zen he would simply raise one finger. His teaching became famous as One-finger Zen.

One of his students decided to ape the master. Whenever one of the other students mentioned Master Gutai this student would simply hold up one finger.

When Master Gutai heard about this he became furious. He cornered the student one day out in the garden. He grabbed the student and, with his gardening shears, cut off one of the student's fingers.

The student was shocked at this and stood holding the bleeding stump and wailing. Master Gutai stopped at the edge of the garden and, looking at the wailing student, took the severed finger and threw it up into the air.

At this the student was awakened and bowed in gratitude to his compassionate teacher.

One-note Zen

Kakua was the first person to study Zen (Chan) in China, yet he never spoke of it so he is not remembered as the first. When he was in China he did not travel but lived way up in the mountains and meditated constantly. If people came to him seeking teaching he would only say a few words and then go further into the mountains, where people could not find him easily.

Upon his return to Japan he lived a quiet life, away from the hustle and bustle of big cities and even big temples. He lived in a very small and shabby temple and did not speak of his travels in China to anyone.

Eventually the emperor heard about Kakua and summoned him to the palace, ordering him to speak about what he had learned from his years in China. For a few moments Kakua just stood before the emperor in silence. Then, just as the emperor was beginning to get angry he pulled out a bamboo flute from his robes and blew one short yet very clear note. Bowing politely afterwards, he put the flute away, turned his back on the dumbfounded emperor and his entire court, and strode away in silence.

Outhouse Zen

A student of Zen had practised meditation for many years, hoping for the flash of insight termed *satori*. Yet, for all his discipline and years of strict meditation, he felt he was getting nowhere. His teacher was no help, repeatedly admonishing the student not to be attached to such experiences. But, one by one, all the other students reached, if not enlightenment, as least some level of true insight.

Finally, angry and frustrated, the student left the temple and went back to the 'world of dust'. On one of his first days there he visited an inn and had a big meal of meat and wine, both of which he had not touched during all his years in the temple.

Later, upon entering the privy and having squatted down to do his business, the sudden plop of his stool falling into the hole below awakened him in one moment to the clear insight he had been working towards for so many years!

Practising Silence

Four friends who had studied Zen for a few years decided to do a silence practice. They all promised not to make a sound, hoping to attain deep insight from the practice. They gathered together one evening and began their meditation. They sat in complete silence, meditating on the 'soundless sound'. As night came on, it got darker and darker in the room. After a long time the oil in the lamps got lower and lower and the darkness became thicker and thicker.

Suddenly one of them called out to his servant, 'Bring more oil for the lamps.'

The next student exclaimed, 'We are not supposed to talk.'

Irritated, the next student said, 'You two are so stupid. Why did you start talking?'

The fourth student said, 'Hah, I am the only one who has not talked!'

They all looked at each other then and burst out laughing.

A Question About a Tortoise

Outside of Master Dasui's quarters lived an old tortoise. Actually it lived underneath the porch of his quarters and had done so for many years. Each day it came out from underneath the floor, made its way slowly to the front of the steps and waited there for Dasui to bring it food.

Dasui always saved some of the greens from his morning meal to feed the ancient tortoise. He loved to watch the animal, with its great dusty shell and knobby legs, moving so slowly and deliberately towards him while he sat patiently waiting, holding the bits of greens in his hands.

The tortoise, once it had made its slow and deliberate way to him, would stretch out its neck, much longer than one could ever guess from seeing the creature shuffling along with its head pulled far back into its shell. Sometimes it even seemed as though it did not possess a head at all, but only four short knobby legs and a small tail, barely sticking out of its dusty shell.

But stick out its neck it would, and once Dasui had placed a bit of food in its mouth, it would pull its neck back into its shell and slowly and placidly chew the food for what seemed an endlessly long time before it would stretch out its neck for another bit.

One morning a student monk was walking by on his way to kitchen duty when he stopped and watched the tortoise and the Zen master in their slow and stately dance, there in the morning sun.

Suddenly he spoke. 'Master,' he said, 'most beings grow their bones inside of their skin yet this being has grown its bones outside of its skin. Why is this?'

Dasui immediately took off one of his sandals and placed in onto the shell of the tortoise. The student stood for a moment, then, realizing this was all the answer he was going to get, continued on his way.

Riding Donkeys

One day the master was teaching his students. 'There are two kinds of sicknesses in the world,' he said. 'One is riding a donkey while looking for a donkey. The other kind is to ride a donkey and not let yourself get off. The first, riding the donkey while looking for a donkey, is a fatal disease. Don't do this! Wise people know this and they have given up the "seeking" disease and the crazy, pursuing mind.

'On the other hand, once you have realized you are riding a donkey yet do not allow yourself to get off, this is the most difficult disease and is usually fatal!

'Of course, you are the donkey. The great earth beneath our feet is also the donkey. How can you ride it? If you continue to ride it you will never cure the disease. If, on the other hand, you get off and don't ride the donkey, all the worlds in ten directions will be open to you. If, by some chance, you are able to get rid of both diseases at once you become empty and are fit to be called a person of the Way and nothing will trouble you.'

Rolling the Dice

Master Huiqin kept six wooden dice in his room. Each side of every dice had only one dot. When he was interviewing students he would throw the dice on the floor and demand, 'Do you understand?'

If the student hesitated, Master Huiqin would drive him from the room.

Teaching Without Words

The master was giving a dharma talk. 'It is important,' he said, 'to know the difference between the inner meaning of words and the words themselves. When we say "fire" there is no fire. When we say "water" there is no water. Your mouth does not burn when you say "fire" and your mouth does not become wet when you say "water". You must remember that fire and water are not themselves words.

'Where can I find a man who has no mouth, eyes or ears who nevertheless speaks the truth, sees the truth and hears the truth?

'One day a monk by the name of Xuefeng went into the meditation hall and started a fire. Then, locking both the front and back doors he began to yell, "Fire! Fire!"

'At this, the rest of the monks began to fear for their lives and cried, "Let us out! Let us out!"

'A monk named Xuansha, who happened to be passing by and heard the shouts of the monks in the burning hall, picked up a piece of firewood and tossed it through the window, whereupon Xuefeng opened the door.'

At this the master nodded at his students, who mostly sat and looked back at him with dull eyes and empty heads. 'Ah,' he thought to himself, 'one day they will understand. One day when they are on fire themselves.'

The Death of a Teacup

Ikkyu, who was destined to become a great Zen master, was very clumsy as a boy. He was constantly dropping things, breaking things, losing things and forgetting things. But his master decided to trust him to clean up after tea one day.

His master had a rare and invaluable teacup. It was an antique and was literally irreplaceable. The young Ikkyu was so very careful as he cleaned and packed away all the tea utensils. But when he picked up the antique cup to place it in its container he accidently dropped it to the floor, where it shattered into many pieces.

Ikkyu was horrified. He considered running away but decided against it. His master had been so kind to him, taking him in when no one else would. He would just have to face the music, he decided, and take whatever punishment he deserved.

But suddenly he had an idea. He remembered something that his master had said in his last dharma talk. When the master entered the room to see how Ikkyu was getting on, he held his hands behind his back.

'Master,' he asked, 'do you remember what you said when I asked you why people have to die?'

'Of course,' said his master, 'that is natural. Everything has its place in the world, a time to be born and a time to die.'

'Well,' said Ikkyu, bringing out his hands and offering the broken pieces of the cup, 'it seems that it was time for your cup to die.'

He did not escape punishment that day but his master seemed to be hiding a smile while he punished him.

The Five Flavours of Zen

Seeing one of his students leaving the monastery, Master Guizon asked him, 'Where are you going?'

The student said, 'I am going to study the Five Flavours of Zen.'

Master Guizon said, 'Everyone else has Five Flavours of Zen. Here I have only the One Flavour of Zen.'

'What is the One Flavour of Zen,' asked the student, whereupon Master Guizon struck him.

Thinking he understood his master's teaching the student shouted, 'I understand! I understand!'

Master Guizon then said to the student, 'Speak! Speak!'

The student hesitated. Now he was not so sure of himself, whereupon Master Guizon struck him again.

Long after that, as the student monk was travelling though China, visiting various monasteries and teachers, he met Master Huangbo and told him of his strange exchange with Master Guizon.

At this, Master Huangbo went into the meditation hall and spoke to the monks there, saying the great Master Ma brought forth 84 people to enlightenment. 'But if anyone asks them about their experience with Master Ma they just wet their pants. Only this Master Guizon is the real thing!'

The Maker of Flutes

The old flute maker left his hut each morning and went down to the river to play his flutes. He usually took along three or four, ones that he had just made but had never played to the river before.

He had got it into his head that unless the river approved of his flutes he would not feel right selling them to anyone. What it was that had given him this idea he was not sure, but it seemed true to his heart and that was good enough for him.

He would sit on a log by the water and play each flute, one at a time. The river would let him know if she liked each instrument – whether the sound was pure and good, and the playing pleasant and pure. And if she did not like it he immediately broke the flute over his knees and flung the pieces into the river, even if he had spent many hours on the instrument. The river knew and she always let him know.

He usually got down to the river early in the morning, before anyone else had gone there. The women washing clothes, the children screeching and jumping in the water, were not there when the flute maker arrived and that's the way he liked it.

It seemed to him a sacred thing, this flute playing to the river. He thought of the river as a mother, really the mother to the entire village. It was easy to see the bright sun overhead as the father. But here, nestled in the morning mist, sitting on a log beside the slowly moving current, he felt embraced by a great sense of motherly love. Being blind, he was more aware of the sounds of the river than many people. He could hear the song of the river playing along with the songs he played on his flutes. He could hear also the wind in the trees, the calling of the birds and the soft sighing of the hills surrounding him.

Even in the deep of winter, when everyone else was huddled round the fire, telling stories and drinking numberless cups of tea, the old flute maker still went down to the river. It was there in the misty river morning, deep in the soft heart of the winter, that he really felt the river playing along with him, coaxing songs from him that he did not even know he knew. But the river knew.

Then, upon finishing playing each instrument, he would pack up his flutes and walk up the many steps back to the village. Sometimes he would meet someone on the path and he would stop and play a tune for them. It was his way of being a part of the village, a member of the greatly extended family that lived there. Often the person he played for would laugh in delight, although once in a while he would draw tears out of them as they listened to his heart song. With his sightless eyes he felt he could see the emotions of the villagers as he played for them. He felt the world all around him in a different way than others, yet he also felt close to them all – the villagers, the river, the birds, even the hills surrounding them. His flutes were his way of communicating and communing with them all, of touching them all, of loving the world around him: his eyes to the world.

The Gates of Hell

A soldier named Nobushige came to Master Hakuin, and asked, 'Is there really a paradise and a hell?'

'Who are you?' inquired Hakuin.

'I am a samurai,' the warrior replied.

'You, a soldier!' exclaimed Hakuin. 'What kind of ruler would have you as his guard? Your face looks like that of a beggar.' Nobushige became so angry that he reached for his sword, but Hakuin continued, 'So you have a sword! Your weapon is probably much too dull to cut off my head.'

As Nobushige drew his sword, Hakuin remarked, 'Here open the gates of hell!' At these words the samurai, perceiving the master's discipline, sheathed his sword and bowed.

'Here open the gates of paradise,' said Hakuin.

The Impatient Student

A young man who had been living an easy and dissolute life came to the master and asked him how long it would take to become enlightened.

'The rest of your life,' said the master.

'I cannot wait that long,' said the student. 'I am ready to overcome any hardship and to become your devoted servant. If I do all of this how long will it take?'

'Probably about ten years,' was the answer.

'That is also too long,' cried the student. 'My mother is old and I need to take care of her. If I work more intensively, how long will it take me to reach enlightenment?'

'Thirty years,' came the answer.

'What?' cried the student. 'First you say ten then thirty! I am willing to work harder than anyone ever has to reach enlightenment. How long will it take me then?'

'In that case, I think you will need to study for at least seventy years. Someone as impatient as you will need that long.'

Sighing heavily, the student bowed to the master and said he would stay.

The student stayed on and studied with the master for some years. He received very little in the way of spiritual teachings. Instead he swept the temple grounds, cooked his master's meals, washed his clothes, and worked in the garden.

In time he found himself thinking less and less about enlightenment and instead found himself enjoying his simple tasks. This went on for three years. At times he regretted giving up his easy life for this challenging one but often he felt that he had made the right decision. The master gave him little instruction, just taught him the basic posture and breathing technique for meditation, which the student faithfully followed each morning and evening.

After three years the master began to give him a little instruction on reading the sutras. After three more years he began to teach him how to chant them. After three more years he began to sit alongside him in his early morning and evening meditation.

Three years after that, the student awoke one morning to find his master gone and his staff, which he always had at his side, leaning against the wall of his small hut. There was also a short note attached to it.

'You are now ready to take my place in the *zendo*', it said. 'I have watched you all these years and have seen your growth and your dedication to whatever task I have given you.

'I can now go back to my home village to pass the rest of my days drinking tea and fishing with no hook. You have attained the level of master. Congratulations!'

The student, a little older and a little wiser, went on to teach other impatient students until he too grew old and went back to his village to drink tea and 'fish with no hook'.

The Master Beggar

Tosui was a famous Zen master. He travelled from temple to temple, lecturing and practising the Way. But he got so famous that wherever he went a large crowd of students and gawkers gathered. One day, when he looked around at all the swarms of monks waiting for him to 'impart his wisdom' he got so irritated that he announced he was done lecturing and told them all to leave the temple and 'go away'. Then he disappeared and no one knew where he was.

But one especially stubborn student searched for three years and eventually found Tosui living under a bridge in Kyoto with a bunch of beggars. He got down on his knees in front of the old master and begged him to 'impart his wisdom' to him.

Tosui looked at him with disgust and finally said, 'If you can do whatever I do for the next few days I might consider it.'

The student was overjoyed. He was finally going to become a student of one of the most famous Zen masters in the country. But although he had put up with many hardships on this journey to find the master, he was not prepared for what happened next.

Tosui told him to take off his official monk's robe and handed him what looked like a pile of rags, telling him to put it on, so he did, but the

raggedy robe smelled even worse than it looked. He was mortified and hoped none of his fellow monks would see him in this terrible state.

Then Tosui told him to follow his lead and off they went to beg for food. Tosui was dressed in even worse rags than the student and smelled just as bad. Whenever they approached someone to beg, that person would jump back from them, holding their nose and most often shooing them away. Occasionally someone would put a few small coins in Tosui's grubby hand, mostly just to get rid of him.

Of course those small coins did not buy much rice and the student felt as hungry after eating it as when they had started out, if not more so. That night, as they prepared to sleep under the bridge with all the other noisy, smelly beggars the poor student felt very discouraged but then remembered that the master had promised to teach him if only he could stand living in the same way as his master.

It took a long time for the student to fall asleep. Around midnight he was startled awake by Tosui shaking his shoulder. 'Come,' said Tosui, 'one of the beggars has died and we need to bury him before the rats come.'

Confronted by that horrifying image, the student became totally awake and helped Tosui to carry the dead man up to a nearby hill where they hurriedly buried him in a shallow grave.

What a miserable way to end one's life, thought the student. To die here under a bridge with beggars and rats.

No sooner had they returned than Tosui announced he was hungry. He went over to the pile of rags the dead man had been lying in and picked some sort of unidentifiable piece of disgusting food and chewed thoughtfully.

It was when he offered some to the student that he backed away in horror. Tosui looked at him and sneered. 'I told you that I would teach you if you could live the way I do for two days, but you can't even last one. Go away and never show yourself to me again!'

The chagrined student groped his way out from under the bridge and took to his heels, never looking back. He comforted himself with the thought that Tosui was no longer a great Zen master but just a dirty, smelly beggar living under a bridge!

The Master Is Defeated

Master Jingqing entered the meditation hall and stood before the assembled monks. Staring at them with great force, he threw down his staff, which clattered to the floor. 'If anyone here moves they will get twenty strokes from my staff.'

Startled, all the monks looked at each other.

Master Jingqing went on, 'If anyone here does not move they will get twenty strokes from my staff.'

No one knew what to say or do. They were all confused and apprehensive. Suddenly the oldest monk there walked up to where Master Jingqing was standing, picked up his staff, and walked out the door, balancing the staff on his head.

'Ah,' said Master Jingqing, 'today, for the first time, I have been defeated.'

The Moon in a Bowl

It was a bright moonlit night and three friends were sitting under the stars and talking about this and that. They had all studied with the same teacher and had many memories to share.

The night went on, the talk went on, until it seemed they had run out of things to say so they sat in companionable silence for a while.

Suddenly one of them pointed to a basin of water that sat at their feet, in which the reflection of the great golden moon could be seen, apparently floating gently on the surface. 'When the water is clear,' he said, 'the moon comes out.'

They all sat there for a few moments, enjoying the moon up above them and the moon below them. Then one of them said, 'When the water is clear the moon does not come out.'

They all laughed over this and then the one who had not spoken suddenly kicked the water basin over, which made them all laugh the harder.

The Tiger and the Monk

Master Baizhang asked his student Huangbo, 'Where have you been?'

Huangbo answered, 'I have been up in the mountains picking mushrooms.'

Master Baizhang asked him, 'Did you see a tiger there?'

Thereupon Huangbo gave out a great roar.

Master Baizhang picked up an axe and made as if to chop Huangbo, who suddenly hit him. 'Ha, ha,' laughed Master Baizhang, and he went to his room.

Later, Master Baizhang entered the meditation room and spoke to the monks there. 'If you go into the mountains you will meet a fierce tiger. You should all go and take a look at it. I myself was just bitten by it.'

The Way of Tea

The great 16th-century tea master Rikyu had studied tea with tea master Kitamuki Dochin as a boy. Later he studied Zen at the famous Kaitokuji temple in Kyoto, where he also studied the Way of Tea.

At the temple he divided his time between the study of tea and meditation. In meditation or when brewing tea he was able to quieten his mind and enter deeply into a state of complete focus on the present moment. Nothing mattered but that one unending moment. Whether it was tea or meditation. Rikyu gave his whole self to it.

He became a famous tea master and had a big effect on the whole practice of *chanoyu* or tea ceremony. Before his time the tea ceremony was performed primarily by the wealthy as an opportunity to show off valuable tea utensils, many of them imported from China or Korea. Rikyu changed all that. Instead of using expensive tea-ware from China he promoted the practice of using rough pottery called *raku*, made by hand instead of on a wheel and thus not uniformly round.

He introduced the use of plain and natural tea utensils made of local wood or bamboo, and criticized the ostentatious tea ceremonies that were popular in the capital, advocating instead a simple yet profoundly deep Way of Tea.

His poem about the Way of Tea became famous throughout the capital.

Though many people drink tea,

If you do not truly know

The Way of Tea,

Tea will drink you up.

To Rikyu the tea ceremony was not just about drinking tea. It was about creating the perfect moment of peace and inner stillness. By giving one's whole attention and spirit to the tea ceremony one could leave the 'world of dust' and elevate oneself into a place of purity and tranquillity.

To Rikyu the Way of Tea and the Way of Zen were one and the same. He posted a list of seven tea rules on the wall of a temple. In one of these he said: 'In the practice of washing the hands before the tea ceremony what is of most importance is the purification of the heart.'

In another he said: 'As soon as the boiling water sounds like the wind in the pine trees, it is time for the guests to enter the tearoom.'

The tearoom or tea hut itself had been created by a Zen priest by the name of Shuko in the preceding century. It was really a very small hut with a fire pit in the centre of the floor. The entrance door was so low that all who entered there, be they noble, priest or even samurai, had to crawl in on their hands and knees, the better to induce a feeling of humbleness, critical for the appreciation of the tea ceremony.

At the back of the room was a small alcove, which was actually the most honoured place in the tea hut. Traditionally there was room for a small vase of flowers or a scroll painting. Upon guests crawling into the tea hut, it was the first place the eye landed and so it was very important to have the right balance of colours and textures there.

Once, Rikyu's patron – the powerful Toyotomi Hideyoshi, ruler of all of Japan – challenged him by placing a large bronze bowl filled with water in the alcove. Beside it he placed a branch of plum blossoms; then he told Rikyu to make a flower arrangement (*chabana*) out of it. The idea was to challenge Rikyu's mastery of *chabana* by asking him to make a flower arrangement out of single branch of flowers.

Rikyu accepted the challenge and, holding the branch of plum blossoms over the bowl, gently shook them so that the petals floated down to the surface of the water, creating the perfect arrangement of flower and water.

To tea masters like Rikyu, Tea Mind and Zen Mind were one and the same. By wholeheartedly entering into the tea ceremony, participants, as in Zen meditation, found themselves in a place of deep spiritual peace and inner stillness.

On another occasion, upon hearing that Rikyu's garden had the most beautiful profusion of morning glories in the capital, Hideyoshi announced he would visit to view the wonderful morning glory blooms. Even though he was a warrior and had worked his way up to his position of great power through much bloodshed, and even though he had once served tea to the emperor himself, Hideyoshi was greatly affected by Rikyu's simple yet spiritually rich *chanoyu*.

He was a great lover of flowers so was excited at the prospect of seeing the fabulous wealth of morning glories in Rikyu's garden. To him these delicate flowers symbolized the transience and changeableness of life.

And so, on the appointed day, Hideyoshi arrived at Rikyu's garden, only to find every flower cut down. Instead of a garden of beautiful morning glories gently waving in the morning breeze, he saw merely hundreds of severed stems.

He was disappointed and furious but kept his samurai composure and turned towards Rikyu, who only bowed and bade him enter the tea hut. Imagine then his great surprise when he crawled into the small space and saw, in the place of honour in the alcove, just one morning glory sitting in a simple bamboo vase!

He immediately forgot his anger and sat quietly, looking at the one flower and letting his mind and spirit become one with that flower.

Wash Your Bowl

A young but very learned (at least in his own opinion) monk arrived at the monastery. He was admitted to the abbot's quarters. The young monk looked at the old man askance. He did not seem very learned (at least in the young monk's opinion). As a matter of fact, he looked like a farmer, like the young monk's own father (whom he had left some years ago). He began to wonder if coming to this rustic temple had been a good idea. (After all, he had already studied under a number of famous teachers.)

The rustic abbot looked at the young monk with a perfectly blank expression. (Perhaps he is deaf, thought the young monk.)

'I have just arrived,' said the young monk, in a loud voice (in case the old abbot was deaf), 'and wish to have some instruction from you.' (He hoped the old fellow had a few words of wisdom for him, though he wasn't expecting much.)

Presently the old abbot spoke up, saying, 'Have you eaten?'

Actually this was a traditional way of saying hello in China and the young monk was not sure how he should answer this. He decided to play it safe and said, 'Yes, I have eaten.'

'Good,' said the old man, 'now go and wash your bowl.'

At this the young monk (who was so full of himself) found himself falling into a great space of emptiness and felt himself expand into silence (and *satori*).

Why Did Bodhidharma
Come From the West?

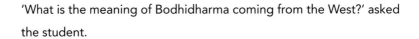

'What is the meaning of Bodhidharma coming from the West?' asked the student.

'One stone in an empty field,' answered his teacher.

The student then bowed to the teacher.

'Do you understand my words?' asked the teacher.

'No,' answered the student.

'Good,' said the teacher. 'If you said you understood I would have had to hit you on your head!'

Wise Words From the Master

One of his (very earnest) students asked Master Shexian, 'What is it that lives beyond the life of the teacher?'

Shexian answered, 'Look how long my eyebrows have grown!'

Another student asked him, 'What is the *dharmakaya* (truth body)?'

Shexian answered, 'In the toilet paper in the outhouse.'

Perplexed, the student then asked, 'What is true wisdom?'

Shexian answered, 'Breaking furniture.'

Another student asked, 'By what light does the master see this world?'

Shexian said, 'His eyebrows.'

'What do you mean?' asked the student.

'Your ears', said Shexian, 'hang down to your shoulders.'

When he was young, Shexian had studied with a famous master named Shoushan. One day Shoushan held up a bamboo comb in front of his students and said, in a loud voice, 'If you call this a bamboo comb you are committing an offence. If you don't call it a bamboo comb then you are not true to what you are seeing.' He held the comb up in front of his startled students. 'Well,' he asked, 'what do you see?'

Everyone was quiet, not wanting to seem stupid, though none of the students knew what to say. Suddenly Shexian grabbed the comb from the master, threw it on the ground, and cried, 'What is it?'

Shoushan looked at him for a moment and then said, 'Blind.'

It was at this moment that Shexian had his first realization.

Notes

[1] Porter, Bill, *Zen Baggage: A Pilgrimage to China*, Counterpoint, 2009.

[2] Price, A.F. and Wong Mou-Lam, *The Diamond Sutra and the Sutra of Hui-neng*, Shambhala Publications, 2005.

[3] Robinet, Isabelle, preface to *Seven Steps to the Tao: Sima Chengzhen's Zuowanglun*, edited by Livia Kohn, Steyler Verlag, 1987.

[4] Barrett, William, ed., *Zen Buddhism: Selected Writings of D.T. Suzuki*, Doubleday, 1956.

[5] Porter, *Zen Baggage*.

[6] Ferguson, Andy, *Tracking Bodhidharma: A Journey into the Heart of Chinese Culture*, Counterpoint, 2012.

[7] Kohn, *Seven Steps to the Tao: Sima Chengzhen's Zuowanglun*, Monumenta Serica Monograph Series XX, Steyler Verlag, 1993.

[8] Towler, Solala, *Practicing the Tao Te Ching: 81 Steps on the Way*, Sounds True, 2016, Chapter 20.

Bibliography

Barrett, William, ed., *Zen Buddhism: Selected Writings of D.T. Suzuki*, Doubleday, 1956

Besserman, Perle and Manfred Steger, *Crazy Clouds: Zen Radicals, Rebels & Reformers*, Shambhala Publications, 1991

Ferguson, Andy, *Zen's Chinese Heritage*, Wisdom Publications, 2011

Ferguson, Andy, *Tracking Bohidharma: A Journey into the Heart of Chinese Culture*, Counterpoint, 2012

Grigg, Ray, *The Tao of Zen*, Tuttle Publishing, 1994

Kohn, *Seven Steps to the Tao: Sima Chengzhen's Zuowanglun*, Monumenta Serica Monograph Series XX, Steyler Verlag, 1993

Porter, Bill, *Zen Baggage: A Pilgrimage to China*, Counterpoint, 2009

Price, A.F. and Wong Mou-Lam, *The Diamond Sutra and the Sutra of Hui-neng*, Shambhala Publications, 2005

Red Pine, *The Zen Teaching of Bodhidharma*, Northpoint, 1987

Reps, Paul and Nyogen Senzaki, Zen *Flesh, Zen Bones*, Charles E. Tuttle Company, 1957

Robinet, Isabelle, preface to *Seven Steps to the Tao: Sima Chengzhen's Zuowanglun*, edited by Livia Kohn, Steyler Verlag, 1987

Towler, Solala, *Cha Dao: The Way of Tea, Tea as a Way of Life*, Jessica Kingsley Publications, 2010

Towler, Solala, *Practicing the Tao Te Ching: 81 Steps on the Way*, Sounds True, 2016

Watts, Alan, *The Way of Zen*, Vintage Books, 1957

Wong Kiew Kit, *The Complete Book of Zen*, Tuttle Publishing, 2001

WATKINS

Sharing Wisdom Since
1893

The story of Watkins dates back to 1893, when the scholar of esotericism John Watkins founded a bookshop, inspired by the lament of his friend and teacher Madame Blavatsky that there was nowhere in London to buy books on mysticism, occultism or metaphysics. That moment marked the birth of Watkins, soon to become the home of many of the leading lights of spiritual literature, including Carl Jung, Rudolf Steiner, Alice Bailey and Chögyam Trungpa.

Today our passion for vigorous questioning is still resolute. With over 350 titles on our list, Watkins Publishing reflects the development of spiritual thinking and new science over the past 120 years. We remain at the cutting edge, committed to publishing books that change lives.

DISCOVER MORE . . .

| Read our blog | Watch and listen to our authors in action | Sign up to our mailing list |

JOIN IN THE CONVERSATION

 WatkinsPublishing   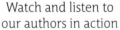 @watkinswisdom

 watkinsbooks    watkinswisdom    watkins-media

Our books celebrate conscious, passionate, wise and happy living.
Be part of the community by visiting

www.watkinspublishing.com